Industrial, Healthcare and Home Cleaning

Industrial, Healthcare and Home Cleaning

Areas that should use this are schools, healthcare,
housekeeping, industrial, factory, churches, shipping,
warehouse, kitchen, dining areas, and home

Sections covered
Bathrooms, sinks, floors, toilets, paper towel dispensers, toilet paper
dispensers, soap dispensers, dusting, mopping, waxing, counter tops,
doors, window/glass walls, furniture, floors, scrubbing, vacuum cleaners
buffers, and urinals

We take no responsibility for anything printed in this booklet

Danger: **Note:** and **Notes:** are suggestions and not intended fo
all procedures or units (use at your risk). **Wear gloves and any other
protective** equipment recommended. If this is supervised, check with your
supervisor for any other directions.
Danger: Not all dangerous situations can be covered in this book, use
common sense

RV 8 1

Index on page 35

Sinks

- **Danger**: <u>Do not mix chemicals</u>
- **Note:** Always follow manufacturer's procedures
- **Note:** Wear personal protection for hands (rubber gloves etc.)
- **Note:** Do not use regular washcloths, paper towels or scrub brushes, they may be too rough for natural marble

Marble Sinks

Natural Marble Sink Cleaning

1. Clean with soft sponge, soft washcloth, Goof Off®, or Steam clean (do not use often)
2. Natural marble is a porous stone, which makes it easier to retain dirt and stains
3. Regular household cleaning products are too abrasive to use on cultured marble, use only a good nonabrasive marble cleaner
4. Never use any abrasive cleaner, green pads, wire brushes, abrasive sponge pads or steel wool
5. Cleaning solutions that work for one stone may not work on another type
6. Be cautious when acidy foods come into contact with marble sinks such as

1. Soft drinks
2. Oranges
3. Pineapples
4. Orange juice
5. Tomatoes
6. Lemons
7. Mustard

Old Porcelain Enamel Sinks With Worn Out Outer Coating:

- **Note:** Wear personal protection for hands (rubber gloves etc.)
- **Note:** When the coating has worn off the media underneath may soak up materials (water, grease and etc.)
- **Note:** Always test cleanser you are going to use for the first time in an unnoticeable area

Clean With Comet®:
1. Wet sink, and put Comet® on it
2. Use a wet rag to cover the sink with a Comet® like paste
3. Wait for about 30-60 minutes
4. Use your paste rag to scrub sink
5. Give the sink a good rinse

Other Ways That Might Help:
1. Clean sink with Magic Eraser®, and a good cleanser
2. Clean sink with green scouring pad, and a good cleanser

Permanent Solutions:
1. Refinish with bathtub enamel as needed (follow the directions exactly)
2. Use Lime-away® or another effective cleanser
3. Replace sink

Porcelain Sinks

- **Note:** Wear personal protection for hands (rubber gloves etc.)

Porcelain Sink Cleaning:
1. Remove any large items from the sink
2. Spray sink with disinfectant spray
3. When feces (dung) is on sink, clean with paper towel, disinfect and continue cleaning
4. Clean mirror
5. Wipe faucet with a paper towel or cloth
6. Clean behind the faucet
7. Wipe sink with paper towels or lint-free rags
8. Clean drain
9. Clean overflow
10. Clean underside of the sink

Stainless Sinks

- **Note:** Wear personal protection for hands (rubber gloves etc.)
- **Note:** Always rub in the direction of polish lines
- **Note:** Unlike traditional sinks stainless need regular cleaning an Delicate care to ensure their surface does not scratch
- **Note:** Small scratches sometimes can be removed with very fine steel wool
- **Note:** If there are smears that will not come off, spray with window cleaner and clean area
- **Note:** Always test cleanser you are going to use for the first time in an unnoticeable area (not all sinks are created equal)

Stainless Sinks Cleaning Media Solutions:
1. Regular = Barkeeper's Friend®
2. Regular = Windex®
3. Regular = Palmolive® dishwashing liquid
4. Regular = Commercial window cleaner
5. Regular = White vinegar
6. Regular = Ajax®
7. Regular = Baking soda solution (two teaspoons per one cup water)
8. Water spots = just rub off with white vinegar
9. Rust = rubbing alcohol
10. Rust bucket = cover with one tablespoon cream of tartar and a few drops of lemon juice, let alone then wipe with wet cloth or sponge

Wiping Materials:
1. Sponges
2. Microfiber cloths
3. Washcloths
4. Paper towels

Cleaning Stainless:

1. Remove any large items from the sink
2. Spray sink with disinfecting spray
3. Feces (dung) clean off first using paper towels and disinfect
4. If there is a mirror to be cleaned, clean at this time
5. Wipe faucet with a cloth
6. Clean behind the faucet
7. Wipe sink with paper towels or lint free rags
8. Clean drain
9. Clean overflow
10. Clean underside of the sink

Never Use:

1. Green pads cleaners with bleach in them
2. Bleach (per most manufacturers)
3. Wire brushes
4. Any abrasive pad
5. Steel wool
6. Any abrasive cleaner

Circular Stainless Cleaning:

1. Remove any large items from the sink
2. Spray sink with disinfectant spray
3. First clean off feces (dung) using paper towels then disinfect
4. Wipe areas with a paper towel or lint-free rag
5. Wipe sink with paper towels or lint-free rags
6. Clean top of the drain
7. Clean overflow
8. Clean panels (if equipped) under the sink

Copper Sinks

- **Note:** Wear personal protection for hands (rubber gloves etc.)
- **Note:** Copper has natural antibacterial agents
- **Note:** Copper sinks patina finish can be damaged
- **Note:** Do not clean with scrubbing, polishing or chemicals

Copper Sinks Cleaning:
1. Drain and wipe with clean mild soap and nonchemical treated clo
2. Rinse with water

Stained Sinks:
Fill sink with regular water and sand with very fine sandpaper (Do not sand areas that are dry)

Do Not Leave Acidy Foods On Or In A Copper Sink:

1. Tomatoes
2. Oranges
3. Lemons
4. Pineapple
5. Mustard
6. Any other acidic food

Cultured Marble (Manmade):

1. Spray cultured marble with a mild all-purpose cleaner
2. Wipe clean with a damp sponge
3. Rinse sponge with water
4. Wipe any excess cleaner dry with a soft towel

Urinals

- **Note:** Wear personal protection for hands (rubber gloves etc.)
- **Note:** When using a bowl cleanser use only in the urinal and toilet bowls
- **Note:** Never use toilet bowl cleaner on flush handles or on hardware (acid will discolor the finish)

How to Clean Regular Urinals
1. Remove any unwanted objects from urinal
2. Clean entire urinal with johnnie mop
3. Let urinal dry on its own
4. Wipe walls around urinal with clean rag
5. Replace consumed urinal block with new one

Waterless Urinals

- **Note:** Has been reported, that chemicals used in waterless urinals, can cause severe plumbing damage
- **Note:** Wear personal protection for hands (rubber gloves etc.)
- **Note:** Do not pour any liquid down waterless urinal trap, it could flush the chemical out of the trap cup
- **Note:** Do not use bleach

How to Clean Waterless Urinals
1. Remove any unwanted objects from urinal
2. Clean entire urinal with johnnie mop
3. Let urinal dry on its own
4. Wipe walls around urinal with clean rag
5. Replace consumed urinal block with new one

First Alternative Waterless Urinals Cleaning:

1. Remove any unwanted objects
2. Spray down the whole urinal with a good disinfect
3. Wipe everything down with paper towel or lint-free rag
4. Wipe walls around urinal with clean rag
5. Replace consumed urinal blocks with new one

Second Alternative Waterless Urinals Cleaning:

1. Remove any unwanted objects from urinal
2. Dip lint free rag or microfiber cloth in approved cleaning solution
3. Wipe urinal completely
4. Wipe walls around urinal with clean rag
5. Replace consumed urinal block with new one

- **Note:** If the person feels they are short on time, they should not wipe off disinfectant too soon
- **Note:** Never use the same cloth on toilets, urinals, and sinks because any undetected feces can be spread all over
- **Note:** For sealant and trap replacement: contact the manufacturer and use their methods
- **Note:** When the urinal backs up, clean and refill the cup per manufacturer's directions.

Toilets

- **Note:** Wear personal protection for hands (rubber gloves etc.)
- **Note:** If using bowl cleaner only use in urinals and toilet bowls.
- **Note:** Toilet bowl cleaner acid will discolor the finish on flush handles, chrome pipes and hardware
- **Note:** Using the wrong chemical can leave smears, rings or spot

Regular Way:
1. Remove any large items from on top of toilet area
2. Dip johnnie mop into a good disinfectant
3. Use johnnie mop to clean top of seat
4. Use johnnie mop to wipe top of toilet and tank (if equipped)
5. Pull seat up with johnnie mop and clean bottom of seat and top of bowl
6. Clean inside of bowl and lip with johnnie mop
7. Clean filler tube
8. Let entire toilet dry on its own
9. To show toilet has been cleaned, leave seat in upright position

- **Note:** If the person feels they are short on time, they should not wipe off disinfectant too soon
- **Note:** Never use the same cloth on toilets, urinals, and sinks because any undetected feces can be spread all over

Alternative Toilet Cleaning:

1. Remove any large items from on top of toilet area
2. Wet rag with approved disinfectant
3. Wipe tank and outside of toilet bowl with approved lint free cloth
4. Clean inside of bowl and lip with johnnie mop
5. To show toilet has been cleaned, leave seat in upright position

Dispensers

Paper Towel Dispenser Automatic (Battery Type)

- **Note:** Wear personal protection for hands (rubber gloves etc.)

Paper Towel Dispenser Cleaning:
1. Remove any solid material on outside of unit
2. If badly stained, apply stainless cleaner on spot
3. Wipe completely with a cloth dampened with stainless steel cleaner
4. If too much cleaner is on unit, re-wipe with a clean cloth

If Not Dispensing Paper Towels:
1. Open unit and push roller button, see if unit will dispense paper
2. If not, test batteries, change if needed
3. See if paper has fallen off holders, reinstall paper
4. Make sure paper was strung through discharge space correctly
5. See if paper fibers have shoved roller from dispense area, remove fibers
6. See if loose paper on side is holding rollers apart, remove loose paper

Will Not Stop Dispensing Paper Towels:
1. Check eyes, clean if needed
2. Change paper towel dispenser

Paper Roll is Jerking/Jumping When Turning:
1. Push roll holder into locked position

Toilet Paper Dispenser Stainless Automatic (Battery Type) Cleaning:

1. Remove any solid material on outside of unit
2. If badly stained: apply stainless cleaner directly on spot
3. Wipe completely with a cloth dampened with stainless steel cleaner
4. If too much cleaner is on unit, re-wipe with a clean cloth
5. If feces is found under unit, clean as needed

If Not Dispensing Toilet Paper:

1. Open unit and push roller button, see if unit will dispense paper
2. If not, test batteries, change if needed
3. See if paper has fallen off holders, reinstall paper
4. Make sure paper was strung through discharge space correctly
5. See if paper fibers have shoved roller from dispense area, remove fibers
6. Make sure paper roll is down on roller

Will Not Stop Dispensing Toilet Paper:

1. Check eyes, clean if needed
2. Change paper dispenser
3. Make sure paper sub roll is not setting off eyes

Soap Dispensers

- **Note:** Wear personal protection for hands (rubber gloves etc.)

Regular Soap Dispensers
1. Fill when needed
2. Wipe unit off with paper towel or lint-free rag
3. If mounted on wall, clean wall around unit when needed

Soap Dispensers Automatic (Battery Type)
1. Check and fill when needed
2. If installed, clean drip catcher as needed
3. Wipe unit off with paper towel or lint-free rag
4. If mounted on wall, clean wall around unit when needed

Battery type soap dispenser problems
Dispenses liquid instead of foam: Change battery
No soap: Replace soap bottle if close to or empty
No soap: If new bottle, prime unit
No soap: If new bottle, reinstall bottle
No soap: Clean the eyes
Dead: Change battery
Dead: Clean the eyes

Soap Dispensers Automatic (Battery Type) on a Counter top

Soap Dispensers cleaning:
1. Clean behind unit
2. Wipe unit off with paper towel or lint-free rag.

Counter top battery soap dispenser problems
No soap: Replace soap bottle if close to or empty
No soap: If this is a new bottle, prime unit
No soap: If new bottle, reinstall bottle
No soap: Clean the eyes
Dead: Change battery
Dead: Clean the eyes

- ## Note: To stop automatic units from turning on while trying to clean sinks:
1. Stand to one side
2. Clean with rapid motions

Sanitary Napkins

Sanitary Napkin - Dispensers

- **Note:** Wear personal protection for hands (rubber gloves etc.)

1. Remove any solid material on outside of unit
2. If badly stained, apply cleaner directly on spot
3. When too much cleaner is on unit, re-wipe with a clean cloth
4. Wipe completely with a cloth damped with stainless steel cleaner

Sanitary Napkin - Collector

- **Note:** Wear personal protection for hands (rubber gloves etc.)
- **Note:** If bag not opened, you may need to remove dirty, stinking and/or bloody sanitary napkins and sterilize collector

1. Remove any solid material on outside of unit
2. If badly stained, apply cleaner directly on spot
3. When too much cleaner is on unit, re-wipe with a clean cloth
4. Wipe completely with a cloth damped with stainless steel cleaner
5. Remove bag and any trash inside unit
6. Open one bag inside the unit

Dusting

- **Warning**: Never start dusting medical equipment screens without asking first (it is best to keep the name of the person giving permission)
- **Note:** Do not stand directly under vent
- **Note:** If Swiffer® has insufficient length, make an extension

Regular Dusting:
1. Use a clean duster
2. Dust all flat and semi-flat surfaces

Ceiling and wall vents
1. Use Swiffer® duster or look alike and dust vent.
2. Go back and forth with the louvers
3. Sweep floor

Floor vents
1. Clean (go over) with dust mop when doing floor
2. If stained, spray with cleaner and wipe off

Vent Cleaning

- **Note:** Areas with more air flow need dusted more often
- **Note:** Wear personal protection for hands (rubber gloves etc.)

If able to remove vent cover
1. Remove all non-fastened solid objects (pencils, papers, etc.)
2. Clean out with a vacuum hose
3. Wipe out with paper towel or lint-free rag
4. Reinstall vent cover

If unable to remove vent cover
1. Use Swiffer® duster or look alike and dust vents
2. Go back and forth on louvers with paper towel or lint-free rag
3. Wipe with damp lint-less cloth
4. Dust all flat areas

Mirrors and Windows

- **Danger**: <u>Do not mix chemicals!</u>
- **Danger**: Do not use razor blades to remove sticky substances from mirrors, the blade can hurt you and the glass
- **Note:** Wear personal protection for hands (rubber gloves etc.)

If you do not have window cleaner solution, try:
1. a small amount of ammonia to water and test
2. a small amount of lemon juice to water and test
3. a small amount of cornstarch (1 Tbsp.) to water and test
4. a small amount of rubbing alcohol to water and test
5. a small amount of dish detergent to water and test
6. One part vinegar to four parts water and test

Spray Window Cleaning:
1. Spray with window cleaner
2. Wipe off with paper towel or lint-free rag
3. Dry with clean lint-free cloth
4. Visually check for streaks, spots and missed residue cleaner

- **Note:** Wear personal protection for hands (rubber gloves etc.)

Rag Window Cleaning
1. Dip cloth in proper solution (Do not apply solution to mirrors)
2. Wipe dry with clean lint-free cloth
3. Visually check for streaks, spots and missed residue cleaner

On window and Glass, if the sticker is already gone and glue is all that is left:
1. Spray with ammonia based window cleaner
2. Wait a few minutes, clean lightly with a green pad or damp rag

If the sticker is still on:
1. Cover sticker with a little oil (vegetable or baby), let set for 24 Hrs.
2. Carefully pull the sticker off starting from a corner

Walls

- **Note:** Wear personal protection for hands (rubber gloves etc.)
- **Note:** Always do ceiling and light fixtures first and complete dusting afterward
- **Danger:** Not all dangerous situations can be covered in this book, use common sense

Wall Cleaning:
1. Dust wall
2. Remove major spots
3. On carpet, put towels down first
4. If possible, turn electric off to outlets
5. Cover outlets in floor with plastic then a cloth towel
6. Start at bottom of wall and work your way up
7. Wash wall with a wall mop
8. On tile floor, mop floor as you go

Furniture

- **Warning:** Never start dusting medical equipment screens without asking first (it is best to keep the name of the person giving permission)
- **Note:** Wear personal protection for hands (rubber gloves etc.)
- **Note:** Never unplug anything
- **Note:** Do not move personal property around
- **Note:** Do not take or remove any food items
- **Note:** Test surfaces before using any new products

urniture Cleaning:

1. Best not to remove objects from top of furniture (unless permission is given)
2. Clean any dirt, debris, and trash from furniture
3. Use small soft bristled brush for tight areas
4. Clean any spills
5. Dust furniture
6. Wipe with furniture polish and do not over wet

Counter Tops

- **Note:** Wear personal protection for hands (rubber gloves etc.)

1. Remove any large items from counter
2. Spray with disinfecting spray
3. Wipe areas with paper towel or lint - free rag

Doors

- **Note:** Wear personal protection for hands (rubber gloves etc.)

1. Dust Door and door top
2. Remove major spots
3. On carpet put towels down
4. On tile floor, mop floor
5. Start at bottom and work your way up
6. Wash with a wall mop
7. Clean door knob then polish
8. On hardware remove major spots
9. Clean hardware with paper towel or lint-free rag

Floors

- **Note:** If you are having problems with residue cut back on amount of cleaning solution in mixture

Ceramic Tile Glazed and Unglazed Floors:
1. Sweep with a non-abrasive bristle broom or dust mop
2. Best to use cleaning and disinfectants designed for your floors
3. Mop with a non-abrasive mop, or one which is designed for your type of floor whether glazed or unglazed
4. It is safe to use a small quantity of dish detergent and hot water
5. Do not add any bleach, abrasive chemicals or harsh chemicals to water

Laminate Tile Floor:

1. Sweep with a non-abrasive bristle broom or dust mop
2. Use cleaner or disinfectant designed for your floors
3. Mop with a proper mix of water and cleaning solution

Wood Floors:

1. Pick up large debris
2. Sweep with dust mop or broom
3. Mop with a proper mix of water and cleaning solution

Mopping

- **Note:** Dump mop water in each restroom drain at least once a week (most drain traps dry out, and this will stop the smell)
- **Note:** For fastest results, use a microfiber mop system

Regular Mopping

1. Fill mop bucket with water and disinfectant
2. Remove all small furniture from mopping area
3. Remove any large trash from floor
4. Sweep floor
5. To mop floor go around edges first, then back and forth until all areas are wet
6. When dry, remove any missed hair on the floor

Flat-Mops

1. **Note:** Fastest way: use flat mops and dry floor with small fan
2. **Note:** Use flat-mops with proper water fill and little or no water will be spilled if bucket tips over
3. **Note:** Flat-mop's harder surface may not pick up all dirt
4. **Note:** Mop dirt/grime to your exit for pick up
5. **Note:** Flat-mops normally don't cross contaminate mopped areas

Flat-Mops:
1. Count number of flat-mops to what will be used
2. Measure correct amount of water to number of flat-mops (pour water evenly on flat-mops)
3. To mop floor: go around edges first, then back and forth until all areas are wet
4. Change flat-mops as needed, and between rooms

Scrubbing

- **Danger**: Very dusty, not for large areas, slow process and vibrations could cause <u>neurological problems</u>
- **Note:** Wear a dust mask
- **Note:** Always mop neutralizer off floor before it dries

Square Non-water Scrubbers are good for:
1. Tight places
2. Corners
3. Wax removal

Normal Scrubbing:
- **Notes:** Do not run over cords
- **Notes:** Never walk through soapy water area into clean areas
- **Notes:** Put down rags/towels to keep water out of other areas
- **Notes:** Always change neutralizer and water when it gets dirty
- **Notes:** If any soap is left on the floor, the wax will flake off

Before Scrubbing
1. Plan ahead and get everything ready first
2. If whole room needs cleaned, clean room first, the floor last
3. Clean corners, edges, and wall boards

Small and Medium Room (1-2 People):
1. Make sure floor is clean
2. Put down soapy water
3. Scrub floor
4. Pickup dirty water with mop, wet/dry vacuum or pickup machine
5. Mop neutralizer on floor
6. Mop with clear water (area needs mopped minimum of two times)

Large Room (3-5 People):
1. Make sure floor is clean
2. Put down soapy water
3. Scrub
4. Pick up dirty water with mop, wet/dry vacuum or pickup machine
5. Mop neutralizer on floor, then before it dries, mop with clear water
6. One or two people follow mopping with clear water (area needs mopped minimum of two times)

Scrubbing Small Hallways (1-2 People):
1. Make sure floor is clean
2. Put down soapy water and scrub
3. Pick up dirty water with mop, wet/dry vacuum or pickup machine
4. Mop neutralizer on floor, then before it dries, mop with clear water
5. Area needs mopped at least two times with clear water

Scrubbing Medium Hallways (4 people):
1. Make sure floor is clean
2. Put down soapy water and scrub
3. Pick up dirty water with mop, wet/dry vacuum or pickup machine
4. Mop neutralizer on floor, then before it dries, mop with clear water
5. Area needs mopped at least two times with clear water

- **Notes**: You can use large barrels instead of mop buckets

Scrubbing Long and Large Hallways (5-6 people):
1. Put down soapy water
2. Scrub
3. Pick up dirty water with mop, wet/dry vacuum or pickup machine
4. Mop neutralizer on floor
5. One or two people follow mopping with clear water (areas needs mopped minimum of 2 times)

Waxing

- **Warning**: Follow manufacturer's directions first
- **Warning**: Make sure you do not wax yourself into a corner
- **Notes**: Make sure you have sufficient wax to finish the job
- **Notes**: Make sure floor is dry before starting
- **Notes**: Some mops look similar to small dust mops and have sealable containers to store them in. These are easier to use, quicker and do a better job

Room Waxing:
1. Mentally section room off, pick an exit to leave from
2. Start waxing in the farthest point from the exit point
3. As you mop wax on, do edges first
4. Do one section at a time
5. Overlap wax
6. Leave the area with the exit point last
7. Wax your way out of the room

Hallway Waxing:
1. If waxing brings you coming back to starting point, start waxing from the edge of your exit
2. As you mop wax on, do edges first
3. Overlap wax
4. Make sure you do not wax yourself from your exit

Vacuum Cleaners

- **Danger:** Never use a regular vacuum cleaner on wet floors
- **Notes:** Use a wet/dry vacuum on wet floors
- **Notes:** Do not run over the cords
- **Notes:** Do not extend cords across active walkways

Rug Cleaning Vacuuming
1. Check to see if bag is full
2. Be sure vacuum is plugged in
3. Push vacuum cleaner back and forth (from you/to you)
4. If available use craves tool for corners and under large low items
5. Empty bag each night
6. Wipe vacuum off before putting it away

Sweeper makes funny sounds
1. Check belt
2. Check roller that belt rides on for any built up debris
3. Check for paper clip in fan or motor
4. See if paper is partly clogging hose or sweeper housing

Sweeper not coming on
1. See if it is plugged in
2. Make sure vacuum cleaner is turned on
3. Check vacuum cleaner frame plug in (if equipped)
4. Check electricity at the plug

Sweeper runs but not picking up
1. Check if bag is full
2. Check bottom of inside of bag for blockage
3. Take sweeper-bottom off, inspect for blockage
4. Check and clean hoses if needed

Buffers

- **Notes:** The norm on pads: the darker the color/the courser the pad
- **Notes:** Make sure you have the proper size buffing pad on the brush (pad driver is under unit)
- **Notes:** Manual high-speed units, you have to push forward and pull back
- **Notes:** Keep moving buffer while energized or you will have light spots from loss of wax
- **Notes:** Do not run over the cords

How to buff:
1. Make sure cleaning of walls and dusting has been done
2. Make sure floor has been swept
3. Make sure floor has been mopped
4. Plug buffer in
5. Spray fine mist of water or buffing solution on floor
6. Some buffers raise and lower handle to go left and right and you push to go forward

Index

This was written by Gary Schierman with a total of 25 years' experience working in elementary schools (as a headman), middle schools (as a headman), high schools (as a headman), warehouse, churches and healthcare facility all in a cleaning capacity.